For Carrie – Christmas, 1988 – with love from Ba-pa and Mama-grand this is a favorite, Carrie, I hope you'll learn to enjoy poetry – Mama-g.

Sun Through Small Leaves
POEMS OF SPRING

With pictures by SATOMI ICHIKAWA

WILLIAM COLLINS PUBLISHERS, INC.
New York and Cleveland

Published by William Collins Publishers, Inc.
New York and Cleveland, 1980.

from *Lilacs*

May is a thrush singing "Sun up!" on a tip-top ash-tree,
May is white clouds behind pine-trees
Puffed out and marching upon a blue sky.
May is a green as no other,
May is much sun through small leaves,
May is soft earth,
And apple-blossoms,
And windows open to a South wind.

Amy Lowell

from *No. 318*

I'll tell you how the sun rose—
A ribbon at a time—
The steeples swam in amethyst—
The news, like squirrels, ran.

Emily Dickinson

from *Pippa Passes*

The year's at the spring
And day's at the morn;
Morning's at seven;
The hillside's dew-pearled;
The lark's on the wing;
The snail's on the thorn:
God's in his heaven—
All's right with the world.

Robert Browning

Awakening

Never yet was a springtime,
Late though lingered the snow,
That the sap stirred not at the whisper
Of the southwind, sweet and low;
Never yet was a springtime
When the buds forgot to blow.

Margaret Elizabeth Sangster

from *A New Year's Burden*

Along the grass sweet airs are blown
Our way this day in Spring.
Of all the songs that we have known
Now which one shall we sing?

Dante Gabriel Rossetti

Here We Come A-Piping

Here we come a-piping,
In springtime and in May,
Green fruit a-ripening,
And winter fled away.
The Queen she sits upon the strand,
Fair as lily, white as wand;
Seven billows on the sea,
Horses riding fast and free,
And bells beyond the sand.

Unknown

from *The May Magnificat*

… What is Spring?—
Growth in every thing—

Flesh and fleece, fur and feather,
Grass and greenworld all together;
Star-eyed strawberry-breasted
Throstle above her nested

Cluster of bugle blue eggs thin
Forms and warms the life within;
And bird and blossom swell
In sod or sheath or shell.

Gerard Manley Hopkins

from *Songs of Innocence*

Little Lamb, who made thee?
Dost thou know who made thee?
Gave thee life, and bid thee feed,
By the stream and o'er the mead;
Gave thee clothing of delight,
Softest clothing, woolly, bright.

William Blake

from *No. 1333*

A little madness in the spring
Is wholesome even for the King.

Emily Dickinson

from *The Child's World*

Great wide, beautiful, wonderful world,
With the wonderful waters round you curled,
And the wonderful grass upon your breast,
World, you are beautifully dressed.

Matthew Browne

from *The Glory of the Garden*

... Gardens are not made
By singing "Oh, how beautiful!" and
sitting in the shade.

Rudyard Kipling

from *No. 1755*

To make a prairie it takes a clover and one bee,
One clover, and a bee,
And revery.
The revery alone will do,
If bees are few.

Emily Dickinson

from *The Green Linnet*

Beneath these fruit-tree boughs that shed
Their snow-white blossoms on my head,
With brightest sunshine round me spread
Of spring's unclouded weather,
In this sequestered nook how sweet
To sit upon my orchard-seat!
And birds and flowers once more to greet,
My last year's friends together.

William Wordsworth

Out in the Fields

The little cares that fretted me,
I lost them yesterday,
Among the fields above the sea,
Among the winds at play.

Unknown

from *Elegy Written in a Country Church-Yard*

Now fades the glimmering landscape on the sight,
And all the air a solemn stillness holds,
Save where the beetle wheels his droning flight,
And drowsy tinklings lull the distant folds.

Thomas Gray

Library of Congress Cataloging in Publication Data
Main entry under title:

Sun through small leaves.

SUMMARY: Presents a collection of poems about
spring.
1. Spring—Juvenile poetry. 2. Children's poetry,
English. 3. Children's poetry, American.
[1. Spring—Poetry. 2. American poetry—Col-
lections. 3. English poetry—Collections]
I. Ichikawa, Satomi.
PR1195.S74S9 821'.008'033 79-23913
ISBN 0-529-05571-6
ISBN 0-529-05572-4 lib. bdg.